How To Find All Missing Persons / Unsolved Cases. And Collect All Reward Offers. Volume XXII. THE CASE OF SHARON ELIZABETH FULTON

DAVID GOMADZA

www.twofuture.world

Copyright © 2024 David Gomadza

All rights reserved.

Paperback **ISBN:** 9798326831859

DEDICATION

To a better future.

CONTENTS

How To Find All Missing Persons /
Unsolved Cases.
And Collect All Reward Offers. Volume XXII
THE CASE OF SHARON ELIZABETH FULTON   1

The Afterlife Conversation

and The Council Of Creation.   6

The Killers.   13

ACKNOWLEDGMENTS

Tomorrow's World Order

How To Find All Missing Persons / Unsolved Cases. And Collect All Reward Offers. Volume XXII. THE CASE OF SHARON ELIZABETH FULTON

BACKGROUND INFORMATION

CASE
CATEGORY
$1m Reward, Cold Cases
DATE
18 Mar 1986
Do you have information about this case?
Your information may lead to solving the crime. Please make a report. You can remain anonymous.
Please quote case number .
Make a report
DESCRIPTION:
39 years of age at time of disappearance.
Light skinned.
165cm (5 feet 5 inches) tall.
Medium build.
Brown shoulder length hair.

Green eyes.
It is unknown what she was last seen wearing.
QUICK CASE FACTS:
Mother of four children under the age of 15 years.
Lived in Duncraig with her husband and children.
Last seen dropping one her young children off in Wangara around 9.30am on Tuesday 18 March 1986.
Had an appointment in Perth that morning and was due to attend a friend's place for a party at 11am, however never attended the party.
Reported missing by her husband on Friday 21 March 1986 at Warwick Police Station.

BACKGROUND:
Sharon Elizabeth Fulton was born in Dubbo New South Wales in May 1946. She was an only child and got married when she was 21, in Brisbane Queensland. Her husband was employed by the Royal Australian Air Force (RAAF) and he was posted to RAAF bases both within Australia and overseas.

The Fulton family moved to Western Australia in February 1983 when Mr Fulton was transferred to Perth through his work and they lived in Duncraig.
Sharon Fulton was the mother of four children under the age of 15 years at the time of her disappearance. She was a caring mother who also enjoyed catching up with friends and was a keen ten pin bowler, competing in local competitions.

CASE DETAILS:
Around 9.30am on Tuesday 18 March 1986, Mrs Fulton left her home address in Readshaw Road, Duncraig.

Mrs Fulton had earlier rung a friend who was having a party at 11am that morning to inform her that she may be a little late as she had an appointment in Perth. Police are unaware of what appointment this was.

At about 11.30am Mr Fulton picked up their three-year old son from Wangara and returned home. Mrs Fulton was not at home when they arrived.
It has been confirmed that Mrs Fulton did not attend the party as arranged and there has been no sightings of her since she left her home address in Duncraig.
Mrs Fulton reported missing to the Warwick Police Station on Friday 21 March 1986.
The person or persons responsible for Mrs Fulton's disappearance have not yet been identified.
If you have any information in relation to the disappearance of Sharon Elizabeth Fulton, her movements around Tuesday 18 March 1986, please contact Crime Stoppers on 1800 333 000 or make a report online below. All reports to Crime Stoppers can be made anonymously if you wish and rewards are available.

https://www.crimestopperswa.com.au/open-cases/missing-suspicious-sharon-elizabeth-fulton-duncraig-wa/

TOMORROW'S WORLD ORDER'S PERSPECTIVES

USE OF PREDEFINED AFTERLIFE PARAMETERS

These guide souls the moment it exist the human body on its journey to Yahweh the creator these define what to do and what to expect as you go to hell or heaven if a souk leaves earth it enters ozone orbit and instantly everything reboots for it to start a new phase of life after living the earth's body now what happens is that it enters the ozone orbit and a simply click caused by the sudden drop of pressure from -1186 to – 20 means the bottom shaft of the soul will lift rapidly and this pushes its back into the air higher than its head best example is a penguin but with real human legs and head just the shape now God created a life predefined program for them instead of asking what should I do and where should I go they instantly know from predefined stencils if you did well and talked most about God then heaven is for you if you did evil and talked more about the devil then the devil is yours now if we Ask what can be of humans without souks this is the answer dead forever your soul is you a new transformation to the electromagnetic waves life where you see Yahweh for the first time and praise him and wish you had seen him a long time ago because of his Majesty and will always be there forever now what are all these you may ask these are rules to be guided by in the creation court in short it has everything humans know about the judges and the presiding judge who will always be Yahweh and 84 angels surrounding the altar 28 high priests who always say Yahweh have mercy on humans and 74 smaller courts priests who always say Yahweh has mercy on humans and 96 princesses who say glory to Yahweh forever and ever amen we have 96 elders who always say if I can why he can't meaning if the devil can drink blood why can't Yahweh who created the devil and blood do the same now this is not the same as saying if the devil can kill why can Yahweh its more on professional grounds rather than challenging now if we look at the inside of the court we have 81 priests surrounding the altar who say Yahweh be merciful to humans but if they disobey you we put hem on trial for you and kill them for you almighty Yahweh inside this is a round circle where Yahweh sits

and asks questions now if we look deep inside the court you will see that there are other things that resemble earth high courts like benches and chairs 10 times human sizes for the gods who are so enormous 2 are equal to 84 billion humans in size
predefined parameters for humans after death as in know what is inside is a large size of books the book of creation is among them with 108978678928367890123486789012458617890 11 pages and is divided into humans first then chapter for animals then a chapter for angles then a chapter for gods and a chapter for Joseph Yahweh's best friend and a chapter for Yahweh's best friend's wife Anna and a chapter for Yahweh's wife Catitighit and lastly a chapter for Yahweh and recently a chapter for davidgomadza as Yahweh's representative on earth marking the new beginnings starting in 2025

1. tell us who killed you
2. tell us what killed you
3. tell us why and who killed you
4. tell us why you died
5. tell us what could have been done and is not done
6. tell us what could be and why
7. tell is when this happened
8. tell us why this is so
9. tell us why this is so
10. what can be done to improve this

What does the book of creation say about davidgomadza David Gomadza is the first and last ruler to be appointed by Yahweh fir the next 25 billion years and will act as his representative on earth deciding cases and upholding his principles on earth and as such has been entitled to 489 trillion dollars in assets this number signifies eternity among humans and the beginning of a new Era chapter 7867892802893862841890287689018320867890123486789018236 487289128610 Creation manual the new Era of new electromagnetic wave conduit signed and dated by Yahweh himself on 27may2024 at 237800 Yatime
creation.universe.ya.start.end.find.davidgomadza.ya.askya.ya

Ask.read.creation.manucreation.universe.ya.start.end.find.davidgoma askya.ya

Ask.rulesofthecourt.start.now.start
David Gomadza welcome the rules of court are guiding principles that tell you what to do and how to do it first you must always say I believe in the court of creation and I shall abide by he rules of this court and shall always do things according to the rules of this court in deciding the cases I am assigned to you must ask what can be done so that you know all your options before making choices the court system will make it easy to check files and ask the outcomes of the decision ask the court the final decision in any case.

THE AFTERLIFE CONVERSATION AND THE COUNCIL OF CREATION'S ANAYLSIS.

I am in heaven I died because of some deadly cancers I can't about but the police especially Pc Thomas asert who targeted me because I was a woman and said I will show you want can be if you mess up with me but I was sure he was joking surely what can a police officer do without bring arrested but I was wrong he had so much power to cover almost everything I met dert who said let's celebrate for the life is ending and I agreed that was my challenge for the day my aty started calculating vitals way so early the day before and said if you want to go to heaven I can make everything ready fast before things go wrong then update when in reception just say I am ready then things will be smooth they just call your name and enter the court of creation through a small hole where you float and said I am here who called me this early but in my case they all said they are really crooks they said it was a test and really literally killed you what kind of a drill is that but never mind that because now they asked questions and started deliberating and said it is a challenge that this case comes to us at a time when earth is so in derail and near peril as everyone takes the law into their own hands to kill and to make things worse to steal

The court had a verdict of misdemeanor adventure that resulted in death because even though she was sick she had years to live according to her long ago but chose to die early and play games with the police but later the court discovered that the police were stealing houses since their formation and never had a single homeless officer and all the woman agreed to to be done on her was proof that they had become the worst that can be this woman to protect her house as her husband died first and the police covered up so that if someone say you killed her for her house then they will say it was left with the husband but in this case Pc Thomas Asert vowed to defend capital gains tax that he won support from the mayor the man who refused a woman to run for the job simple because the job demanded more walking and traveling then she was okay she had no problems but after this incident her hip swelled and never healed until day of death when the mayor Edward stomnop said if it was not for cancer she could have been a great doctor but I mean mayor and all said who are you talking about the killer or the victim years after she died someone said the mayor to cover his tracks ran to her doctor and said imagine if I am to be found that I discriminated a woman just because she is a woman and not on talent then what would have been me then without your radiation if we check if any radiation codes detected it is 08983876589028678018367890284 9

How To Find All Missing Persons / Unsolved Cases. And Collect All Reward Offers.
Volume XXII. THE CASE OF SHARON ELIZABETH FULTON

SHARON ELIZABETH FULTON

this case presents challenges never met before in any case using electromagnetic wave 89284286789285082872867890184218310263186519210 this woman was murdered by a man called astern ajern who said what can be of wholes with no money but with bills to pay and strangled her then took off all her clothes and dumped her in the streets but then went back to collect her and cut her into pieces then feed her to the pigs but one of the pig died and was taken to the butcher were a human hand was discovered inside it but the police refused to come because the butcher was known for wasting police time he took pictures and sold them to the news paper who printed them but denied to say whether they were real or not but said they could be real if you ask the butcher but the man tasked with the injury hated the butcher and kept quiet until someone found a human leg in the bin with an ankle bracelet but took the bracelet and threw the leg in the woods until another time when another found an ear badly decomposed with a diamond and took the earring and said today i become the worst thing ever stealing property of the dead but then again i am human if the cops can't bother searching for her then what now let's see what this case entails this case is about humans not caring enough but to end up choosing property rather than the search of the truth if we ask what all this means this is the answer Yahweh works miracles and must be respected when the case started a wo0man had bet that she can easily tell everyone if she is murdered but all will choose to ignore the tale tale signs and might actually steal from her now this day she woke up and said if i can then what but if they can't then what this day she looked well than some of the days as she was suffering from cancer she said my last day according to this aty so i will go to town and do the things i always do and ask if anyone wants one great sex for the road and she said okay then she left and went to town and met a man named astern ajern real name thomas noptrt who said since the two say its your last day to protect your house from thieving police probably the ones who killed you

How To Find All Missing Persons / Unsolved Cases. And Collect All Reward Offers.
Volume XXII. THE CASE OF SHARON ELIZABETH FULTON

using doctor atert stert real name dr tortet who might have administered the drug why can't we enjoy life tether i can do with a friend and last sex is always out of this world so i heard and she smiled and said i want my house to be in your name for 10 years then sell it and give the money to cancer charity as per aty then he said thank you what about mine do you want them to come for me too and they laughed and he said if we can then why can't they do last orders at the bars but what about after why not make it interesting so i go with a bang so that you all talk about me when i die he said okay then they started drinking alcohol before a man said i heard you already died the police are at your house removing your body then they looked lost and said what and he said they had a tip off you want to run away and die in the bushes to protect the house but sergent atert optert real name thomas wants the house for his family and if you don't die in there then what she looked lost and devised a plan and said if they want to take my house then let me do this and you must obey if you are serious about the house after sex strip me and put me in a blanket and take me to the street leave me for 2 hours and after that come for me and and remove me then cut me into 10 pieces and place me in the streets at these points but put in with jewelry so that a person removes jewelry and hand in the flesh as proof i died in the woods after all this then go with this part and give it to the police and take the house after that day a man was seen carrying a carpet with a human body inside and someone rung the police but they said that person keep phoning complaining about everything then another rung and said he saw a human leg with ankle bracelet but they dismissed this report then another came and said he saw a human hand inside the pig and called the police then the butcher took photos and placed them inside the newspaper of the 10th of may 1986 but were assumed as fake otherwise the butcher could have sent this to the police whether they liked it or not lastly he took her pelvis and said i found this near where i live i had a woman died and she left the house in my name this is the proof and gave them but they said the case is mistaken with another the case in question the body was recovered in the house two days ago when you were seen drinking alcohol with another woman then he sat down and looked lost and said okay i go take the house but one day

How To Find All Missing Persons / Unsolved Cases. And Collect All Reward Offers.
Volume XXII. THE CASE OF SHARON ELIZABETH FULTON

someone can find the truth and what will happen is that the house will be mine then and they all laughed and said why didn't you come with her so that we say she run away from us but death is knocking so we guard her and he said but that stealing what is the difference with real crooks you are crooks in uniform and what can be of crooks like you in this world and they all laughed he left and never seen again as someone said he murdered his wife for her house and walked in the police station with the pelvis and they said it wasn't human now if i look at this case its a case of misdemeanor because a person who wants to protect her own house must do so at any cost the police have become thieves using all tricks to steal her coordinates are 08983678901894802867890123489012486789018428618928410819026483
sharon fulton 08983867898720983867890284185286789013867890 south of queensland in a pit with animal or pig remain there is a leg with a bracelet that says cancer patient 08967890284 her number now looking at this number her doctor was dr astern ajern real name asortep sotetet who said is she can escape then where can she go they will steal bring her here to her house but if she is clever she might set them up for the world to know the truth that they steal houses not even one of them is homeless yet even the prime minister of queensland erdostep at one point was homeless they finished everyone with a house all killed in broad daylight if it wasn't for aterstuvwxyz which i have against them they could have targeted me as well meaning a court verdict that bans my house to be taken by the police in queensland now if we look deeper sergent thomas stertp said if they can't give us protection let their houses protect each and everyone of us for we need protection all they had to do is ask if they want us to stand for them and say yes then we automatically get a 10 percent pay rise and a house deposit of 15000 each but we struggle on minimum wage of 2.67 pence per hour in 1986 this is just an insult which will be rectified when your god comes to the rescue because we will say if we can protect everyone then we can act for all and lead the way and take houses from weak women who will die from disease like alopecia malignant or cancer not just cancer but cancer that let you run from the house and say the police take this

How To Find All Missing Persons / Unsolved Cases. And Collect All Reward Offers.
Volume XXII. THE CASE OF SHARON ELIZABETH FULTON

house i don't want the disease is too much i can bear the cost of the disease let alone the house strip all clothes and die in the bush but we come in because we know the reason why you did it is because so that we don't get the house but we are clever we simple say a jane doe meaning for 20 years no one can claim to know this person when we all have failed that means after 20 years the case is closed and only god can come and change that and even if he come he has to show us her dna so that we match to the evidence we have otherwise there is no case by then will have sold the house at a profit 4 times the value i bought the house for of which i can actually tell you that the price to be put up is 2098762 that is 2mill dollars but we get on contractual credit meaning we don't pay a thing not even a deposit but 20 dollars to say i like it the force signs the papers that it's ours but that's all now if we ask what they say about this case then this is the answer it is one of the notorious cases of all time on that the police especially pc thomas sertp took drastic steps to avoid real evidence because he wanted the house so much he turned away almost everyone except jtert real name stertopqrstuvw meaning astert who lives in avern who said if you can't process tge evidence then that's stealing but he said okay what do you have then he said a piece of her ear with a stud with initials str meaning sharon elizabeth fulton and he said how come str stands for sharon elizabeth fulton and he said i said i have a stard that says sef who is sef to you insist her the owner of the house you just bought for 20 dollars because a week for one to die and 2 weeks for you to be in that house is murdering god himself because how can you hide that evidence god presents on arrival on reception then if this continues then i will be forced one day to come as well and take it from you and this is speaking for everyone because police are not thieves are they and he said they are not but str and sef are different things because when she left her earnings were tge sef and what you brought here are the str meaning a different name so if you excise me i have a job to do and he said how do you know all that yet you named her a jane doe and he said i can prosecute you for planting evidence and kill you myself for threatening me and walk again and he said why again he stopped and said my legs were so hurting and look how i can walk now he looked at him and left but 6 years later he killed him

How To Find All Missing Persons / Unsolved Cases. And Collect All Reward Offers.
Volume XXII. THE CASE OF SHARON ELIZABETH FULTON

[calculate dna sequence for sharon elizabeth fulon ready ttstuvwxyzrrtuvwxyrtstuvwxyt]
then he said if we can then we must but then he smiled but he was shot at the spot but his partner pc atertop mnop real name usltver retpon who said who gun down a police officer for a house and live no one then a tear after this incidence the house was sold for 22789786 to a bank meaning 20000000 20 mill profit which was given to the police housing association as his wife died of the same cancer as sharon elizabeth fulon then all said justice has been restored one crook police officer can get everyone blamed for stealing we kill too police thieves
the end

sharon elizabeth fulon who died of cancers of the pelvis bone that literally fell and she said if life can like this then what if not death what else and drunk beer called jack daniel's then so much and took a cocktail of pills in front of thomas ersert who said its all about controlling the pain and fear of death but after that everything becomes okay if we ask what had happened this is the answer she was shot by the hospital at birth with a secret chip code 28786789078678902867890234810983684412490 that was manufactured by deloitte in disguise as part of a detergent agent but known as a dieurgent chip code 76890 that revolutionized death in the early 1960s then widely used in rich stubborn women who owned big house but with vaginas who fall off easily meaning who are likely to lose the house now then things were different than now where even the police have to look for their own accommodation then they would rely on the housing association with long waiting lists then if you wanted a house you would find a victim and give the force a job with a case so hard to solve that it being on the list will create a buzz as people talk about it that encouraged officers to ignore evidence so that they label the person as a jane doe meaning an unknown who don't own property this is how they ended up possessing the property now if we ask what happened to this house pc thomas esert said if it can be taken its now or never capital gains tax will be forward but as the same value in 5 years or 8 years depending if the value go to the target which is the 20 mark 20

How To Find All Missing Persons / Unsolved Cases. And Collect All Reward Offers.
Volume XXII. THE CASE OF SHARON ELIZABETH FULTON

million value 20 years which ever comes first after only 5 years the bank offered 28789786 for it and another police officer who owned it took it there and sold it for cash reducing the value by 1 million for instant deposit and he fled the country but was found dead weeks after before he spent much but the money was never traced again after that

THE KILLER, THE CONFESSIONS AND THE COORDINATES

Was killed by a lethal injection administered on 27 of March by a simple code sent from a police office in Queensland street at number 8 which used to be a police office in 1986 the year she died but later changed after that means Pc Thomas asert killed her for the house which he later bought for 20 dollars.
Pc Thomas sertp was involved in the death of a woman called Sharon Elizabeth Fulton who owned one of the biggest houses in town and said who then runs this town you tell me the police who we all know steal houses from orphans runs the show not in Queensland as long as I stand I will put a word to the mayor to see that these this is so or sack all these retarded that's who think a woman in a dress will never run this county I put in my name for the mayor position after Fulton failed as an alcoholic but as a woman these that's started whistling saying if she can they I can but then I lose a job to her but then who look after the community prior to that and after is it her or us the police a police officer called Thomas asert said what can be done with wholes that own big mansions they will lose if they can't pay the bills of such a huge mansion above all with a vagina that can fall if too much dicks pound on it to raise money for bills he then said I can take this house fairly and square if there was a God I would say God I like this house but then keep all to myself he looked at Pc aternop who said then what became fully we stand firm against dirty policemen like and stopped as Pc Thomas asert lifted his rifle from the desk and said she was shot her doctor said cancer of the pelvis

How To Find All Missing Persons / Unsolved Cases. And Collect All Reward Offers.
Volume XXII. THE CASE OF SHARON ELIZABETH FULTON

but can take forever to die and he growled and said what can be done to speed up things his aty in front of Pc aternop said it can be speeded up faster I have a code 8928367890248678902841856789 0823 now if we Ask what this code does is to awaken the devil in cancer by screaming I am hungry all the time until day of death reducing life to a quarter from day introduced Pc Thomas asert smiled and said but how do I send it and aty said say send dot this code to [ ] then dot send and he said that and a beep like sound said received but shelved then he said empty everything and ask what can be done to increase things and his aty said say what if but then when he said that the other cop tried to punch him and said you bastard why all this for a house why not work hard I mean smarter but then again the fact that you joined the force is a fact that you can't think but steal is worse you spoil all of us covering for you and he said get transfer and go everyone is down with it a house and fir you 12 % after 5 deal or no deal and he said what do you take me for you will see in 5 if this deal goes through what I will do to you and he loved and said too much ujeujeuje go and get laid oh it's you humping a diseased woman to death and he screamed I will kill you one day that's my mum I mean and looked at him with evil eyes and walked away

Now his coordinates [Thomas asert] are 0898267890183678902384871028 6798234810264 in a grave marked Pc Thomas asert the one to serve all but beloved wife aunice Pc anerop is alive at these coordinates 0898386789028487890123486789 02848012389018678902841923617 80123862841789068 his phone is 07928386789027723108789284 in Queensland

Coordinates for Sharon Elizabeth Fulton

sharon elizabeth fulon who died of cancers of the pelvis bone that literally fell and she said if life can like this then what if not death what else and drunk beer called jack daniel's then so much and took a cocktail of pills in front of thomas ersert who said its all about controlling the pain and fear of death but after that everything becomes okay if we ask what had happened this is the answer she was shot by the hospital at birth with a secret chip code 2878678907867890286789023481098368412490

Coordinates of the chip buried inside a pit with bones with DNA sequence XXTERTUVWXYZRTSTUVWXRTUVWXYZTTROP Meaning reindeer shot by Pc Thomas asert on 29 may 1986 at the travel lodge astropq where he said aa woman found bones of a human being but Pc Thomas asert said if it were human then he would have asked Pc anorp to check but dna sequence suggested a reindeer instead so a reindeer it is later he said if there is a God only God would know that the bones are not all humans we are not going to cover these up but test if there is a good as required by nster who said what if there is a God but no0w if we look at all these cases they are after answers the killings etc are not to test God but to trick to test God but collect vital information in order to build the world's first God computer that can imitate God so that it matches exactly what God does if he were here that way then there is no need for the real God because the computer will do the same even better

…I found God…visit www.twofuture.world

THE CLAIM

the reward offer

THE COLLECTION

www.twofuture.world/donate

ABOUT DAVID GOMADZA

visit www.twofuture.world

signed david gomadza
ask.davidgomadzaauthorised.licensed.checkya.askya.ya

04 June 2024 22.04pm
scotland
00447719210295
davidgomadza@hotmail.com
info@twofuture.world

www.ingramcontent.com/pod-product-compliance
Lightning Source LLC
Chambersburg PA
CBHW032312240526
45464CB00023BA/2996